Feeling for Infinity

Clare McDonnell

SUMMER PALACE PRESS

First published in 2006 by

Summer Palace Press
Cladnageeragh, Kilbeg, Kilcar, County Donegal, Ireland

Printed by Nicholson & Bass Ltd.

A catalogue record for this book is available
from the British Library

ISBN 0 9552122 2 7

This book is printed on elemental chlorine-free paper

for Susan and Jessica

Acknowledgments

Some of the poems in this book have appeared in:
Envoi; Outposts; My Native Donegal; Kent and Sussex Poetry Folio; Women's Work; The Cork Examiner; Poetry Ireland Review; The SHOp; Leitir; Donegal Culture and *Donegal News.*

They have been anthologised in *A Deeper Light* and the Errigal Writers' two publications: *Beyond the Rubicon* and *Brass on Bronze*, and on their CD, *Eleven Ways to Kiss the Ground.*

Biographical Note

Clare McDonnell grew up in England but has lived in County Donegal since 1978. She is a founder member of the Errigal Writers and has read in the Poetry Ireland Introductions series; the Irish Writers' Centre; the Errigal Arts Festival; Cúirt Poets' Platform; Word of Mouth, Belfast and Rathmullan Summer Festival. In 2003 she won second prize in the Samhain International Poetry Competition. She gained a M.A. in creative writing from Lancaster University through the Poets' House in Falcarragh in 2002.

CONTENTS

Intruder   11

Insomnia in a Strange City   12

Per-verse   14

Slug Feasting   15

Muckish Mountain   16

Maggie   17

Breakfast with Salvador Dali   18

Wild Strawberries   19

Diagnosis   20

Labyrinth   21

Riding the Wave   22

May Time Woodland, County Donegal   23

Haiku   24

After-comers   25

Hay   26

Dawning   27

Gale Force   28

Coming Through   29

Birthday Party   30

Nocturne   31

Passion   32

Planet Earth   33

Drop   34

Water on Mars   35

The Boulder   36

Once, she thought of killing him   37

Power Cut   38

Cliff Edge   39

Seen from Above   40

Extremes   41

Still Life   42

The Three Bears   43

Barbara Hepworth Sculpture   44

Maps   45

Shadow   46

Merman   47

Sunbeam   48

Carraig Lough   49

Rhinoceros   50

Label   51

Flying   52

Crossing   53

Dark Matter   54

Wing   55

Rain   56

For Dympna   57

Delayed Gratification   58

Into injury time   59

Dances with Leaves   60

Strawberries   62

Letting Go   63

The End   64

Intruder

My startled daffodils
are trumpeting their alarm.
Someone has been in my house.
I can sense his touch on the doorknob.

His footfall has bruised the silence.
The creak of floorboards
has woken the moth at my window,
disturbed the mouse in its sleep.

His shadow has darkened my table,
spilled into my china cup.
He has seen the fly in my cobweb,
the dust on my blue vase.

He has smelled my morning coffee.
He has read the titles of my books,
met the eyes of my photographs
and received their smiles.

His breath is in the air that I breathe.

Insomnia in a Strange City

Too hot with the duvet on,
too cold with it off,
I am a corkscrew, twisting
on the edge of wine-dark dreams.
The territory is scented by others,
making an intruder of me.
Tired of watching each red minute pass
I go to the window, look the city in the eye.

A tethered dog barks twice
to ask if he is alone in the world.
There is no reply.

Jaundiced light bleeds over the pavement
and spills into oily puddles
that splash the worn shoes
of a lame night-walker.
Macho youths bluff their way
past shadows in doorways.
A Coke can dances along the gutter
to its own tinny music.

A tethered dog barks twice
to ask if he is alone in the world.
There is no reply.

Lovers, whose fermented hurt explodes
through the black bottle-neck of night,
scream their grief at each other.
A coiled cat unwinds itself
into an arch, then settles again
on yesterday's dead headlines.
An alarmed car, molested by a stranger,
shrieks in panic for its owner.

A tethered dog barks twice
to ask if he is alone in the world.
There is no reply.

Then suddenly dawn sighs
and a blackbird sings of home.
I crawl under the alien duvet
and crush the poking fingers of insomnia
that teased my tired mind.
In splintered dreams of dark streets,
I run to comfort the tethered dog.
We lie together in our chains.

Per-verse

Funny how sometimes
the world doesn't rhyme
and the rhythm is strangled,
comes in short sharp blasts,
is not quite as you
expected it to be
and there's always that perfect long line that doesn't fit in any-
                                                                    where.

Until a leaf jitterbugs by,
the river explodes into glitter,
the gutter runs with gold
and a middle-aged couple
hold hands on the street.

Then suddenly – harmony
of shade and light
space and time
rhythm and rhyme.

Slug Feasting

When I rattle the biscuits for the cats
does he hurry in his slow slug rush,
his elastic reach, towards the sound or smell,
hoping the cats will leave him a morsel?

He's here now, nosing a kibble along
in front of him, trying, as it rolls and twists,
to get a grip on it, to bite or suck or lick it.
Will he give up, look for easier prey?

In his slow-motion hunt, his struggle
to overpower it, he secures it against a wall.
His soft mouth closes over the nipple-like end
and he lies there feasting until he falls asleep

and his green-marbled body contracts
into a dark hump, the kibble soft with saliva.
When he silvers himself away into the night
he leaves a Celtic design on my doorstep.

Muckish Mountain

Yesterday she sulked under her blanket;
today she has cast it away,
is feeding off forget-me-not blue.

Close up, intimate as never before, we touch.
Her skin, brindled with shale, does not flinch.
Her breath comes in gentle gusts.

But when I round her back I see,
under her obdurate haunches,
mechanical maggots eating at her flesh.

Maggie

In memory of Margaret Sheridan

She peoples the house with the long-dead.
They mill around her, friends and relations,
unchanged by time or death. They share secrets
and stories with her, as she unlearns the present.

Now she sits by the turf fire where once
she dappled her legs, baking soda bread;
where she looked after aging parents
and made tea for raking neighbours.

She, who has to be lifted out of bed
and cared for like a baby, is always preparing
to go to Mass, cycle to a wake, churn butter,
milk the cow, carry in the turf.

Then, between whispered rosaries, she pleads,
I want to go home! She's ready for the road,
her suitcase packed with certainties,
waiting until her mother comes to fetch her.

Breakfast with Salvador Dali

I could see right through him
as he arrived on a row of bicycles.
He wanted something to eat.

He helped me cook pancake
watches and tossed them
all over the kitchen.

They drooped over
the backs of chairs,
over branches of trees

and dead fish, they slithered
off the edge of the table.
He shaped butter and bread

into buttocks and breasts,
with legs in strange places.
He ordered an egg on a

dish, without a dish,
and when I gave it to him
he hung it from the ceiling

on a rope. He looked
at the pancake watches
and said it was time to go.

But part of him didn't want to go,
so he left that part behind,
propped on a forked stick

balanced over a shiny slice of water,
suspended like a hammock
from wall to invisible wall.

Wild Strawberries

I was picking wild strawberries
when Neil Armstrong stood on the Moon.
I put my foot on the Earth
carefully, between the delicate plants,
and plucked the tiny orbs, red and juicy,
changing the destiny of their seed.

Diagnosis

In the hospital ward,
amongst bellows-rasp of lungs,
born-again-lovers hold hands
over the white sheet.
They gaze wordlessly into the past,
searching for something to cling to
in the black ocean of their shock.

Outside, the woman sees
beautiful, clear-skinned schoolgirls
lighting secret cigarettes.
Her horror leaks into her face.
They jeer in whispers as she passes.

Labyrinth

I dare not look down.
The dark tunnels go deep;
sweat-slimed walls,
petrifying cold,
terror congealing on the tongue,
echoes of sighs and snorts
and unidentified cries.

My bull-headed fear lurks there.
The vibrations of his anger
rise through the ground
and travel up my spine.
I cannot face his stiletto horns,
his naked animalness,
his ferocious eye.

Riding the Wave

I wish I could catch a wave
and ride it to the shore.
A wave with a silver mane
tossing in the wind,
an arched neck
of turquoise marble, melting.
I wish I could tame it
with whispers,
feel its spittle on my face,
taste the salt of its sweat,
become one being with it
in an explosion of white
crashing on the sand,
breaking to a bubbling,
a susurrating shine.

May Time Woodland, County Donegal
for Jessica

That rock-breaker has been banging
into the bone of the hill for nineteen days.
Delving, splitting its petrified marrow,
exposing Mesozoic strata.
The iron jaws of the excavator
have spat out mounds of smashed rock.
The skyline is utterly changed.

Oak trees have been wrenched from the ground.
They lie in cataclysmic heaps,
naked roots obscenely splayed,
ancient arms snapped off at the elbows.
Leaves, responding to the call of spring,
are wilting on broken branches.

There is no sign of the soft-necked bluebells
or the creamy flowers of the wild strawberry.
Gone are the dawn-bright primroses
that clung to the slope so recently.
The lowlight violets, wood anemones,
and the starry celandines are all extinguished.

Where have the chaffinches gone,
full of eggs, their half-made nests lost?
What happened to the hedgehog,
newly woken from his warm, brown leaves?
Now that the shrews and voles
are crushed under the feet
of today's *Tyrannosaurus rex,*
what will the secret owl hunt?

Haiku

mist-silvered cobweb
oak leaf in a still puddle
autumn's first footprint

~

how light the petal
lies in the palm of my hand
my knowledge of you

~

the sky has fallen
silently into the lake
clouds float with lilies

After-comers

After-comers cannot guess the beauty been.
Gerard Manley Hopkins

the fierce bright beak of a blackbird excavates
the humus for worms his slender toes graffiti the
mud with hieroglyphs that only palaeontologists
will be able to explain when they dig them up as
fossils and try to imagine a past when birds flew
free in undefiled air chorusing in an abundant
world that still nourished a rich profusion of
trees when flowers with unnameable shades of
petal still flourished emitting long-forgotten
perfumes when lovers could walk in the
benevolent rays of the sun treading shoals of
daisies underfoot could stand in the shade of an
oak tree and finger the ancient wrinkles in its
bark when the earth was beautiful unbroken and
steady as the eye of a blackbird in its tiny orbit

Hay

It's a honey-coloured autumn afternoon.
I go to buy hay for my goats,
drive onto a farm over dry, rutted fields.
The farmer and his sons sprawl in the shadow
of a long rick of baled hay, eating take-away chips
and swigging from cans of Coke.

I wait in the car while they finish their meal.
I don't want them to hurry;
I enjoy the innocent smell of hay,
sun on my arm, the swish of tails of amber cattle
in the next field. I remember how it felt
to have sweat on my brow and the thirst it brings,

how good tea tasted from a corked bottle,
how we devoured chunks of soda bread
spread thickly with farm-made butter,
in the shade of a newly made haycock,
and how the horses browsed while they waited
in the meadow buzzing with insects and energy.

We squeeze three bales of hay into the back
of my car, and one into the passenger seat.
Juddering towards the road,
I drive on the cusp of a rut.
I switch on the car radio. It is three o'clock,
the eleventh of September, two thousand and one.

Dawning

The sun is a blur in the Turner sky.
Grey brushstrokes straddle the valley.

      The ravenous chainsaw roars,
      loudly devouring the woodland.

Spiders have spread their silken cloths
from spike to spike on the glistening whin.

      The excavator groans and clunks
      chewing mouthfuls of world.

The wren springs from stone to stone,
her twinkling song rings down the ivy-curtained wall.

      Make straight the way for houses,
      the field's hungry, final crop.

Gale Force

Last night a storm
tore through the trees.
It soughed around the house,
knuckled at the window,
howled under the door.
It was full of passion,
intense, overwhelming.

Today, it is exhausted.
Beech trees stand
in pools of copper confetti;
the wan smile of the sun
lemons the bark of the birch,
belies the night's extremes.
Your glance is casual.

Coming Through

A breeze, smooth as cream, cools my cheek;
each blade of grass is heavy with dew;
the blackbird shawls the dawn in music;
the wood is soothed by cooing pigeons;
noisy starlings return to nest in the eaves;
the robin flits close by, jingling his song.

Ewes stand, eyes closed, suckling lambs
that nuzzle and butt skin-warm udders;
angular cattle line up by the gate,
their breath steaming from moist nostrils;
the dog turns her belly to the pale sun and sighs;
the old donkey has come through another winter.
I feel again what I believed impossible.

Birthday Party

I spilt my jelly, tripped over grown-ups' feet,
could never think of anything to say,
and the lace on my dress chafed my neck.
I was always polite, tried hard to win
at musical chairs and hunt the thimble.
My party piece was 'The Lamb' by Blake.
With cheeks burning, I stumbled through it
and rushed back to sit on my unruly hands.
When it came to my turn to blow out
the seven coloured candles and make a wish

I always wished to be back in Ireland
on my Uncle Jerry's farm, with real lambs,
to finger their curly coats and hold bottles
for the orphaned ones who suck so fiercely.
I wanted to hide in the hay barn with Shep,
hunt for turkey eggs under nettles,
follow the bony cows at milking time
and be allowed to carry the candle upstairs
to the big bed with a bolster down the middle.
I just wanted to be at home.

Nocturne

Taut tonight – I need tree music.
I escape into the stormy dusk,
wade through a galaxy of daisies.

Firs are ocean in the gush of air,
crashing on imaginary shores;
redneck sycamores shout,
gesticulating with broad hands;
beech trees lisp, whisper
and dance to sibilant music;
ashes shake their purses
of adolescent seeds;
birches shiver and gasp,
grasp their flimsy dresses;
sabre-toothed holly battles
brittle and unyielding;
gorse bends low to scratch
and comb the ragged grass.

My unease softens. I stand,
face upturned to a petal-storm of stars
and the silver seed pod of the moon.

Passion

The inevitable desert stretched before me,
unwavering footprints behind.
I stumbled upon an oasis, palm trees, olives,
and a cool deep well of bright water.
My parched lips longed for the forbidden drink,
for the tangy flavour of passion fruit.
I filled a sparkling vessel and sipped tentatively,
drank my fill until my throat was numb.

Thirst sated, I slept one hour, dreamt of a garden.
On waking, I found the shadow of a tree
darkening the well. A fence of thorns,
so lightly stepped over before I drank, now
entangled my ankles, broke my skin. An after-taste
of vinegar, an aroma of hyssop, tainted the air.

Planet Earth

Relentless gravity
is the leash that ties her
in the Sun's back yard.

She is weary of the fouled
space she patrols, weary
of scratching her mangy skin

over-run with parasites
that bite, burrow,
corrupt her flesh.

Her wounds fail to heal,
she is losing her rhythms,
her seasons, her sanity.

She dreams of escaping
to cavort with the stars,
to bathe her burning skin

in the cool Milky Way.
But her howls go unheard
in the vast blackness of space.

Drop

My boat
is motionless on
a looking-glass lake. A
drop of water, suspended from
the edge of the oar, holds a miniature
sun at its heart, an upside-down world where
time has stopped. Stopped: for as long as the
stillness between two beats of a moth's wing,
the silence between two notes of a thrush's
song. For as long, in the scale of things,
as we have inhabited   this drop
of water, suspended from the
edge of the cosmos.

Water on Mars
for Susan

Mars has the memory of water
carved into her parched rock.

Does she remember rivers;
their silkiness, their languid drawl,
their flux and gush, their roar,
clots of frogspawn, green weeds waving?
Did she understand the pebble talk of water,
delight in the twinkle of sun and shade
and the sudden shimmer of fish?

Was there once someone there
who saw a lake as flat as a polished table,
the surface so tense that insects hardly
dented it, darting between lily pads?
Did he notice how wrinkles halo out when
a swallow dips for flies, or how the breeze
strews handfuls of sparkle over the water?

Was there an enormous ocean there
whose curled tongue was shredded on rocks?
Did it suck the sand from beneath a poet's feet
leaving him in unsteady wonder?
Did his child cup handfuls of spilled sun
from its surface, let it seep through her fingers
to become water again, licking her ankles?

In winter, did rain slap him with glass hands?
In summer, did it finger his face softly,
bring back aromas to dryness,
plump up the wall's cushion of moss?
And when it stopped, did each lupin leaf
hold a diamond between its fingers,
was the fissure a stream, did the red rock steam?

The Boulder

They had been close
but a boulder fell between them.

Each tried to hide it
from the other,

to spare the other
the weight of it.

Each tried to carry
more than their share

but neither knew
what the other side

of the boulder was like.
Often, they thrust

sharp edges into each
other's bleeding hands.

Because they pretended
the boulder was not there,

neither cried out in pain
or showed their hurt to the other.

Eventually,
the boulder became so large

that they could not see over it,
or touch each other any more.

So, when it crushed them,
each was alone.

Once, she thought of killing him

he was cutting logs for the fire,
splitting them in half.

He raised the axe above his head,
brought it down viciously
into their white fibrous flesh.

Two pieces were held together
by a scalp of moss.
He ripped them apart

and hurled them into the barrow.
The sap that bled from them
had an acrid scent.

Anger crackled out of him;
an electric charge
seeking earth.

Power Cut

Between the boiling of the kettle
and the pouring of the tea,
everything stopped.

What if it had been my heart
stopping, the sun exploding,
or the earth ceasing to spin?

Is that how it was for Kimiko,
singing as she worked in her kitchen?
Between the boiling of the rice

and the feeding of her child,
everything stopped
on that August day in Hiroshima.

Cliff Edge

I am up on the cliff
where the breeze is fresh on my cheek
and the sky is seagull-soft.

Below me the grey mist is swirling
hiding and muffling the pounding of waves
that break and shatter on the black rocks.

The rocks and the sea want me.
They would wash me, push me, smash me,
until all the pieces of me were smooth

like the pebbles they worry ceaselessly.
If only I could see the black rocks
and the waves' white bleeding,

their thunder would not frighten me so,
I would not keep dreaming of them
and feeling their spray in my sleep.

I would not have to come each morning
and listen to them, at the edge of the cliff.

Seen from Above

Aerial photograph by Yann Arthus-Bertrand

At first glance
it looks like wallpaper with straight rows
of white specks on a green background.
If you look closer
you can see that the white specks are crosses
standing on smooth grass
and if you look closer
you can see that each cross has a black
shadow of grief attached to it
and if you look closer
you can see writing on every cross,
uniform, unique,
and if you look closer
you can see flowers fading at the crosses,
no more footprints in the dew,
and if you look closer
you can see the future.

Extremes

A desert woman trudges all day to fetch water.
She carries it home on her head
and measures sips into her children's mouths
through cracked lips and the lethargy of starvation.
Their eyes hold no hope of anything better,
no memory of a quenched thirst. Her cattle,
protruding bones, shrunken udders,
are dying around her, the crops withering

while I stand in the shower each morning,
water cascading over me, down the drain.
I fill my glass from the tap, water flowers,
use washing machine, flush toilet, wash car,
make fountains and pools in my garden:
uncounted sips, mouthfuls, jugs of water.

Still Life

Look at the blatant roundness of the apple.
See its sleek polished skin,
how light bleaches the topmost surface,
shadow enriches the blush underneath.

See the arch of the stem with its tiny mouth,
empty of the branch's nipple
where it clung and honeyed all summer,
and the dent where it enters the fruit –

a young girl's voluptuous belly-button.
Apple sheen borrows a patch of purple
from the full-cheeked plum
where their smooth skins kiss.

The stubby stalk of a pear
reaches for the stars –
chubby child at the back of ballet class,
trying so hard, bruised so easily.

They are all embraced by a hand
of bananas in a glint-edged bowl
on an oak table in an old farmhouse,
while the ochre evening slows to stillness.

The Three Bears

I had a teddy bear called Clare,
Michael's was named Michael,
the baby one was Francis, like our brother.

One day, at a teddy bear's picnic
on the gingery-brown carpet,
I remembered our visit to the zoo.

Two chairs on their sides made a cage.
I put the bears into it; they couldn't get out.
They sat there staring through the bars.

Their eyes were vacant, looking beyond me,
like the eyes of the real animals;
like the eyes of the leopard, whose soft paws

traipsed up and down, up and down
on the concrete floor, while shadows of bars
slid along his back, first one side, then the other.

Something plummeted inside me.
I snatched the three bears from the cage,
clamped them to my chest,

kissed them one after the other.
And I hugged Clare.
I hugged her and hugged her and hugged her.

Barbara Hepworth Sculpture

I want to walk around it.
I want to see it from
every side, look
at it full on,
at a slant
eyeball
to eye
hole,
skin
onto
stone.
I want to
stroke, slide
my hand into the
curves, through the
cleft that looks beyond;
want to   feel the silken
smooth   -ness under my
fingertips,   to glide the palm
of my hand   across swellings
and hollows; I want to rest my
touch on it, 'til I draw out
the cold – let it live.

Maps

Last night's green bottles stand all day
on the table. Their shadows move slowly
across the meridians on the open atlas
as you start to turn the world under your feet.
A clot of wine dries in the heart of your glass,
your abandoned shoes trip me, your Beijing
address, stuck to the fridge, unsettles me.

I too, step off the edge of my old map
with its straight lines, exact directions.
I let go, jump into an unmarked landscape,
an unwritten snowfield, and hope
my footing will be as sure as yours.

Shadow

My shadow flicks between
the wooden palings of the fence,
disturbs the bee at its intricate work,
interrupts the butterfly
showing her wings to the sun.
My shadow arm embraces every tree I pass,
fingers stroke every flower
and do not bruise the petals.

This other *me* is more pliable.
She floats in pieces on water,
she wrinkles on wrinkled sand,
climbs steps squarely before me.
She walks through café windows
and sits with tea-drinking strangers.
Sometimes she falls over a cliff,
remains unhurt.

My shadow *me* is shameless.
She nestles her head
on the shoulder of the man I covet.
Her shadow lips touch his,
so lightly that he does not feel them.
And look – where our shadow selves
lie together on the grass
daisies ignite between us.

Merman
for A. H.

I feel the ocean pulsing through his veins.
It crests and troughs with his every breath.
I can taste the salt spray on his lips.
The heft of his moody tide delineates my day.

When he turns tail, makes for the bare rocks,
stirs the wrecks and corpses in his depths,
my night begins. I am stranded on damp sand
among crabs and broken shells, to await his return.

But oh! When I see him materialize from waves,
how the dawn-shine of his face starts my day!
How his kiss soothes my parched skin!
How he buoys me up – how he fills me!

Sunbeam

The solitary prisoner
focuses his day
on a fine beam of light
that sneaks into the cell.

He follows it
as it creeps across the floor.

He dips his fingertips,
bathes his hand in it,
lets it pool into his palm.

He rotates his hand
so the hairs standing
on his cold skin
catch the ray as it climbs
the blue mountains
of his veins, slides
and curls around his fingers.

It is the umbilicus
which ties him to the world.

Carraig Lough

I am under your spell.
I want to melt
into your mercury
as an otter melts into water.
I want to smell the breath
of the lilies you wear
on your breast,
feel your skin dent
under the fingers of the wind,
watch your thousand eyes sparkle
when the sun smiles at you.
I want to be cradled
against your brown heart
where I can lie and gaze,
as you eternally gaze,
at the clouds in the blue
and the stars in the black.

Rhinoceros
for the Errigal Writers

O look! It's a rhinoceros –
a rhinoceros with wings.
He's flying in a red sky.
His square head exudes joy,
his feet kick in ecstasy
at being weightless.
Cool air spirals between
the folds of his thick skin.
His wings are strong,
streamlined – almost elegant.

He doesn't know what spell
made them grow. It might be
something to do with the words
he plays with in his mind –
how they mix and match,
soften or sharpen each other,
how they spark sometimes
when they touch,
set off a chain reaction
that reaches beyond reality.

Label

I was labelled when I was young,
like a new-planted rose
or a calf with its ear-tag firmly fixed.
I could see what the label said
reflected in other people's eyes.

No matter how hard I tried
to pull it out, deny its existence
or change the wording on it,
I could not succeed.
It grew into me – I into it.

Flying

I sit in my seat and prepare to die.
My tight-clenched hands squeeze out salty wet fear
as the air-whale monster in which I'm entombed
awesomely roars in my ear and my brain.
The world shrinks as we climb cloudy tresses,
speed to transparent paths paved with sky.
With each choke of the engine, each whim of the wing,
I expect to plummet. Time stalls, flounders on
until gravity seems to be getting its way.
We tilt, slowly sink lower and lower.
The star-stitched runway arches to meet the wheels.
We bump down. My eyes feast on solid ground.
The red rubber band of my fear snaps.

Crossing
for Lisa Steppe

Could the droning plane
that made my windows shake
in the bleak London night
have been the same one that shook
yours, hours later in Dresden,
before it dropped its bombs?

Now, a lifetime later,
crossing on the Rathlin ferry,
over the inky ocean of history
we connect, exchange
our twin-born memories,
fears that still limit our lives.

Dark Matter

mysterious   fearful   untouchable
a thing that is   yet seems not to be –
plasma that fills the space
between the planets and the stars
no smell no taste no texture
no name no equation
so basic to the cosmos
yet so invisible so vast
our minds cannot conceive of it.

what kind of darkness is it
is it like the fathomless pitch of the soul
or the coaly pupil in a mouse's eye
or the blackness filling an underground cave
that has never known the presence of light
and only spawns white blind creatures
are we the white blind creatures of space –
as they lack eyes   do we lack some organ
that could perceive the now imperceptible?

how thick is it   how deep   how still
is the speed of dark greater than the speed of light
how much must there be to contain a universe
what if it started to seep into another dimension
would we and all the planets go with it
or would we stick in the throat of a black hole?

Wing

In the doorway of the barn
I met a swallow – his lightning flight
so accurate that I didn't even feel
the wind of his wing as he wheeled,
screeching, over the lee of my shoulder.

Rain

The sky bursts its bag of water.
On a high wave of anger we rise,
crash apart on a rock of difference.
The man who loves rain is going.

We wait for a bus that never comes.
An unexpected drive. In aching silence
we follow a truck hauling two broken cars.
Then that other cloudburst.

Hollow house, twelve socks on a radiator.
A sudden closeness, frozen words melt.
The clean, sharp-bladed pain gives way
to wonder at such a gentle breaking.

For Dympna

The word

came out
with such force
that my tongue
was too slow
to stop it.
My teeth snapped
but its tail slid

between them.
Your eyes
widened,
your lips clamped
on a gasp,
trying to keep out
the taste of it.

Sorry
crept up my
throat, sidled
out of my mouth,
limp and feeble,
not able
for its task.

Delayed Gratification

During long summer days
raspberries plumped;
each tiny seed was cushioned
in juicy red flesh. They stained
and scented my fingers
as I placed them, sun-warm,
into a clean white bowl
that blushed at their touch.

I postponed the pleasure
of crushing them on my tongue.
Autumn now, and I rediscover
the bowl, dull and crazed.
And I mourn for the fruit
dried to a scab at its heart.

Into injury time

with grating hip
creaking back
blurring eyes
and an incontinent

memory –
all endings
no beginnings
amputated love
punctured soul
and a very confused

muse –
one last chance
to score that perfect

poem.

Dances with Leaves

Leaves tap at my back door.
When I open it they hustle in,
dance in circles around my ankles,
scuttle across the tiled floor.
I close the door and they freeze
in a chance game of statues.

An oak leaf lies on its back,
paws up like a pup,
or the empty hand
of a sleeping child.

A glossy holly leaf
stands, stiletto-heeled,
a lady dodging puddles,
a reluctant goat in a gateway.

An ivy leaf, face down,
sticks to the floor in a damp kiss,
its tail straight up, a cat
who knows his territory.

Dry beech leaves become coiled
barley sugar, or the twist
inside a half-eroded shell
washed up on a shore.

Slant sunlight elongates
their shadows, highlights
their Barbara Hepworth curves,
their stilled gesticulations.

I want to see them move
so I open the door
and they pirouette
in a wild choreography
governed by their shape,
their embrace of the air.

Sweeping them out
against the wind is like
trying to stop the words
of a new-found poet
lodging in my mind.

As I sweep out one scattering,
another blows in.
They crouch in corners,
hide in shadows;
they whisper to me in my sleep,
leave their taste on my lips
when I wake.

Some always elude me
and when I rediscover them,
mingled with my own words,
I know there's been a mating,
something new conceived.

Strawberries

I was writing a poem about wild strawberries
when I heard that the Queen Mother was dead.
Memories of a black-and-white world crowded in:
newsreels of her walking through the smoking
remains of blitzed and broken London; rationing,
busses burning, people sheltering in tube stations;

and the two princesses my mother extolled
as an example for me to live up to;
the impossible expectation that, one day,
we might be invited to the queen's garden party
to stroll in the sun on a striped lawn
among men wearing top hats and medals,
ladies in broad-brimmed hats and long gloves,
eating strawberries and cream.

Nights with my head under the blankets
feeling the vibration from heavy bombers
droning overhead towards Germany;
and the chug, then the silence, then
the shriek of the doodle-bugs as they fell
and exploded all around us, and Mummy
telling us next day whose house had gone,
who had to be dug out, who was dead.
No wild strawberries in those bleak days.

Letting Go

A moth is growing old on my window.
A fragment of mottled muslin, he hangs
until I ease him onto my hand
and cage my fingers around him. Outside,

I unlock them. He falters on my palm,
stunned by the brightness of freedom.
I blow softly on his wings
and he goes, zigzagging into the air

as if measuring the sides of a glass case,
testing edges, feeling for infinity.
You and I unlock reluctant fingers,
falter on the palm of parting.

The End

You know when you're there.
The yacht has docked.
The flaming sunset is over.
No more lightning bolts.
No more islands to discover.
No more depths to trawl.
You might as well disembark.